Bloodroot

Bloodroot

poems

CATHERINE JAGOE

SETTLEMENT HOUSE

Library of Congress
Control Number
2016951272
Jagoe, Catherine
Bloodroot
ISBN 978-0-9859468-8-3

First edition
Manufactured in the United States of America
Cover design and illustration by Ellen Hamilton
Typesetting and composition by Sarah Fannon

SETTLEMENT HOUSE

PO Box12004
Silver Spring, MD 20906
www.settlementhouse.us

ACKNOWLEDGEMENTS

My thanks to the editors of the following publications, in which these poems first appeared, occasionally in different versions and/or titles.

Atlanta Review, "Solstice Under Snow" / *Comstock Review*, "Bloodroot" / *Contemporary American Voices*, "The Dogs of Love" and "As If" / *diode*, "Gardening" / *Driftwood Review*, "Migrants" / *Hospital Drive*, "Onset" / *Nebo*, "Still Day Here" / *North American Review*, "Arctica Islandica" / *Poem*, "What Men Want" and "Elementary School" / *poemmemoirstory*, "Eyebrows" / *qarrtsiluni*, "Psalm" / *Red Wheelbarrow*, "Hummingbird"/ *Rockhurst Review*, "Mermaid" / *The Innisfree Poetry Journal*, "Prisoner of War" / *The Yalobusha Review*, "To My Parents on the Day of the Dead" / *Verse Wisconsin*, "The Breath of Houses" and "Lily" / *White Pelican Review*, "Kite."

"Drafting" first appeared in *Poetry Jumps Off the Shelf*, an anthology edited by Shoshauna Shy (Woodrow Hall Editions, 2004).

"This is the Blue," "Wisconsin Wedding Party," "Drafting," "Maple Keys," "With Child," "After Birth," "Wellspring," "Man in a Parking Lot," "Excavation" and "Her Guide to Household Management" appeared in the chapbook *Casting Off* (Parallel Press, 2007).

"Hummingbird," "Kite," "Psalm," "Bloodroot," "Solstice Under Snow" and "Arctica Islandica" appeared in the chapbook *News from the North* (Finishing Line Press, 2015).

"The Bargain" received the Norbert Blei Poetry Prize at the 2015 Washington Island Literary Festival.

"Burial Ground" won the Joseph Gahagan Prize at the 2016 Milwaukee Irish Fest, under the title "Cillini."

My thanks to Larry Moffi for believing in this book and my deepest gratitude to Alison Townsend and the Lake Effect poets—Marilyn Annucci, Robin Chapman, Susan Elbe, Jesse Lee Kercheval and Sara Parrell—for helping to birth it. Also, always, to my early teachers, Malcolm Powell and Lawrence Garner. In fond memory of the late Daniel Kunene, professor of African Languages and Literature at the University of Wisconsin-Madison, for his encouragement and his luminous example of how to be an internationlist poet/translator.

CONTENTS

Three: Bloodroot

Coda

Notes

I come of those . . . who taught me that we
could both be at home and be foreign.

—THABO MBEKI, "I Am an African" speech (1996)

I've wanted only to sleep and dream and wake
in some country my heart could call home.

—CECILIA WOLOCH, *Carpathia* (2009)

[O]ne of my ambitions, perhaps my governing ambition, was to belong fully
to this place . . . to be altogether at home here. But now I have come to see
that it proposes an enormous labor. It is a spiritual ambition, like goodness.
The wild creatures belong to the place by nature, but as a man I can belong
to it only by understanding and by virtue. It is an ambition I cannot hope to
succeed in wholly, but I have come to believe that it is the most worthy of all.

—WENDELL BERRY, *The Long-Legged House* (2003)

home /həʊm/ *n., adj., adv., & v.* 1. The place where one lives permanently, *esp.* as a member of a family; a fixed abode; a windy house on a hill; but what if there is no such place, if one is of No Fixed Abode or of many abodes which are all fixed while one ricochets between them; the sharp smell of your mother's hair as you pull the brush down her scalp, slowly, slowly, and she sighs a long sigh. 2. The place or country of one's origin; *esp.* the British Isles; the place where you grew up / the place where you are always a child. 3. The dwelling place or retreat of an animal; the place whose peculiar odor you do not perceive except for a piercing moment, returning to it after a long absence. 4. Any place of residence or refuge; the place you crave when you are tired or sick or otherwise disarmed; the place where people do not ask *Where are you from?* 5. A place or region to which one naturally belongs or where one feels at ease; or not, always not quite altogether. 6. A place where a thing flourishes or from which it originates. 7. An area where a player is supposed to be free from attack. **home ground**: an area, locality, or subject with which one is intimately familiar; **home truth:** an indisputable fact, especially one associated with a wound; **homelooseness**: a feeling of foreignness; the perpetual presence of absence; **home-making**: (re)creating a household or dwelling place through poems; **to drive home:** *fig.,* to penetrate into a person's feelings or consciousness to the maximum extent; **homing**: capable of returning home, usually over a great distance.

One

Passport

Passport

I am your distant
relation from a one-time mother
country. About me you know
only my names, familiar
and unpronounceable.
You have not shared
the railway carriages
I've sat in, their seats'
itchy plaid nap thinned
by other travelers' thighs,
or paced with me while waiting
at departure gates. You
cannot see the white scar
on my wrist, the chilblains
on my toes, or smell
the coal-fire odor
clinging to my clothes.

A tall, stiff woman.
The one with earplugs
in her bag, light glinting
off her glasses, a gaze
that's guarded. The kind
who wants to have her cake
and, yes, eat it, too. That sort.

I translate the transatlantic.
My back is hunched
from all the baggage I have carried,
checked and unchecked—
for which I've paid high fees,
my paraspinals taut as piano wire.

My worldly goods were shipped from England
to America in wooden tea chests, foil-lined,
a half lifetime since.
My shoes were full of tea dust.
Books too, for years.

Believe me when I say I never meant to stay.
I pray to the god of second chances, doors,
chameleons, coyotes, migrants and divided loyalties.
I'm hefted to the hills, the borderlands.
I'll be your go-between.

If anyone goes looking for me, tell them
I've gone to earth.
Tell them this time
I'm traveling light.

Eyebrows
In memory of my grandmother

Did you know your eyebrows
have taken root in me and grow

dark and determined and bushy and more
incongruous the older and grayer I get?

I thought myself a different race.
You adored the Silver Jubilee, Thatcher,

the empire, the England of tinned prunes
and bungalows and Mr Kipling cakes.

You were fat, fond, foolish,
fearful, but you taught me to sing

"Waltzing Matilda" with all my heart,
and to hell with the unsentimental.

You taught me sweet: how to lick
condensed milk off the lid of a can

without cutting my tongue. Dignity
and its lack: the prolapse, the chamber pot

under your bed, Mars Bars stashed among
the condoms in the top cupboard.

The gut-twist of remorse when we left you
alone with your hanging baskets by the sea,

your black cat, Percy, and the photos
of the jaunty pilot you met on a bus and married—

dead all too soon—and the favorite daughter
born in India, lost in Egypt to TB.

Aging was alien to me then, but loneliness,
leave-taking already a language I was learning

each time we piled into the car and left
you sobbing by the hot and tarry road.

Crossing the Welsh Border After a Transatlantic Flight

Red dragon rambling on the road sign.
The story in my mouth is full of luscious gutturals.
The color of this country is somewhere
between dun and loden. Lichened gravestones
listing in the graveyard in Llangollen.
Winter here is muted, dank, dark, dripping.
ARAF, reads the road: *Croeso i Gymru.*
As silent as breath, the fields of staring sheep.
Dinas Brân, tall one, I hear you calling.
What is it that leaps up on the threshold,
twisting dear and painful like a broken bone?

Viroconium

Hadrian's wish, this lavish city built
in quiet and wind and cold

to bring home to the Celts in their thatched huts
the grandeur, the magnificence of Rome;

this outpost, so far from the olive groves,
the turquoise dazzle of the *Mare Nostrum*.

Walk down this lane, once military highway
running from coast to hinterland.

These stubs of red-brick walls, these arches held
the grunts of weightlifters, the splash

of heated water, the slaps of the masseurs
on oiled flesh, the hubbub of the market,

the legionaries' jokes, the cries of vendors,
the arguments of merchants talking politics.

Look up: a rim of hills—old hump-backed Wrekin,
Wenlock Edge, Long Mynd, Brown Clee,

the Stiperstones, where slaves mined for lead,
and beyond, Snowdonia, the rebels' redoubt.

This road, these walls, this city, beacon
that petered out in 410, after the legions left.

Silent by the Severn under the hills'
soft, unmoving gaze, it sat. The outdoor pool—

a folly in this climate—filled up with rubble.
The mosaics cracked. The Dark Ages

came and went, and brambles, nettles, moss,
the detritus of time and living matter.

A bowl of sky,
loud with the baaing of sheep.

Stand still and listen.
Reach out through the wind

and touch the echoes.
You will not be here long.

Burial Ground

They still call, those unlived lives
of the unbaptized, stillborn, unshriven
before death and buried in unhallowed ground,
no headstones to mark their graves.

Always after dusk the hospital van
arrived at Belfast's Milltown cemetery
with its load of dead infants
who were slung, unsung and coffinless,
by a sour-faced grave-digger
into an open hole.
A few still bore their caul.

Elsewhere, in the country, it was the fathers'
job to bury them, at night, after
the chores, the fodder forked
over half-doors, the lamps swung
through muddy yards, the steaming pails
milked from the cows in their stalls.

Men numb or grim or weary bore them
out beyond the last houses, to where
snipe creak and the sheep bleat,
to a patch like this on the other side
of a wall, where a track leads up the hill
and a stream comes down. They would
take their spades and pierce
the sod beneath the clumps of rushes,
furze bushes, bramble, nettles,
a hunch of wind-warped thorn.
It had to be done before the dawn.

Sometimes they laid them lovingly,
limned in pebbles of white quartz.
But no one's to know: to the eye
of the passerby there's just rough,
lumpy ground, tussocks of wet grass.

Babies lingered in limbo—in eternal
darkness, but no actual pain,
like floating in a *currach* on the outgoing
tide at night, minus your oars,
through cloud-burst, peat-drench, soak,
snow, drizzle, and the louring clouds;
the mist, some days, descending over all.

Enigma Variations

The vinyl records that are left
are stacked in attics now, collecting dust,
along with the gramophones,
and maybe only I recall the task
I had each day for school assembly
in the gym, to choose the record,
lower the delicate, heavy tone arm
with its tiny diamond thorn
onto the spinning black disc,
to orbit the image of a small white dog,
his head cocked at the brass mouth
of a horn, revolving slowly
in the center.

If I felt shaky, having been mocked
or jeered at for my Home Counties accent,
in need of majesty and cymbals, I'd put on
one of Elgar's marches, wait as the album hissed
before launching into *Pomp and Circumstance.*

When my unbelonging felt less raw,
soothed by a girl who sometimes stroked
my braids in line, I'd choose his *Enigma Variations,*
strive to drop the needle on the exact groove
of the violins' wistful, tremulous G, linking
numbers eight and nine, the start of "Nimrod."

I was between eight and nine myself
and "Nimrod" moved me deeply—
something about the longing in it.

Vinyl is coming back, I hear, preserving
and transmitting sound through time so accurately.
But Nipper, the famous terrier
on the record label HMV: *His Master's Voice,*
was listening attently to his *late* master's voice,
even then already gone.

A lifetime later, on another continent, I sit inside my car
transfixed, transported, listening to "Nimrod"
on the radio—how it surges, aches,
broadens into great, glowing vistas,
capturing the ceaseless movements
of the human soul. Elgar,
the announcer says, wrote the *Variations*
as sound portraits of those he loved the most,
but the cryptic, hidden theme of all of them
is loneliness.

Shropshire, 1974

Wood-pigeons wake me wooing in the greening
dawn: "Take *two* cows, Hughie, two."
My window's scoured with rain and thrush-song.
The milk van clinks and stops, then wheezes on.
Rising, I scan the distant mountains mired
in cloud, lather Imperial Leather in the sink,
wash my strange, new, sweet-sour pits and sex,
apply the cream deodorant named Mum.
There's not much time to eat or put my armor on.

Our heavy door squeals shut behind me.
The early morning air is tender, raw. Downhill,
the Brownlow Arms still smells of last night's booze.
Thick-set, laconic men in rubber boots
with hands hard-bitten from manhandling ewes
emerge from the newsagent's with the *Sun*.
Sixteen-year-olds in Crimplene bell-bottoms
push squalling infants to the launderette.
I quail and scurry on, pretending not to look
at what I could become.

I shrink from boys slouching to the Secondary Mod
beneath the weight of satchels and the sacks
of coal or carcasses they'll one day shoulder;
the shrill girls, blue-lidded, sniggering,
in platform heels and bare, chapped knees.
I in my tie and blazer, intent on catching
the bus at 8:19 to somewhere bigger,
I with my *Hamlet*, Latin, Milton,
cannot meet their mocking eyes.

I only know a negative: not this, not this—
not Fabdec, the dairy, early motherhood,
with perm and market basket, puffing Dunhills.
I want more, but what? I stew in misery
ad nauseam and traipse unseemly distances,
roaming the meres, fields, coppices, and lanes,
alone and always hungry, pockets crammed
with windfalls—small, hard, cankered pears.
I do not want to push a pram. Who do I think I am?

Mermaid
For my mother

You always were the first one in,
splashing gamely, drawn to swim,
wading with little screams of fear and pleasure
into rivers, streams and mountain lakes,
deep, dark bowls of bone-bare slate,
while startled sheep bounded away.
There is your voice, high squeal,
exhorting your reluctant kids to come *on*
into the pebbled murk of the North Sea,
while pensioners in parked cars doze
and men with knotted handkerchiefs
around their heads lie shivering by windbreaks.

You always wore a swimsuit that you donned
awkwardly, behind a towel, leaning on us
to balance on one foot.

We thought we knew you.
Yet still, sometimes, when you were out,
we searched your room. One day,
our father's sock drawer held a photo
that had never made the family slide show.

Green gorge in Africa, white water
sluicing off your skull
and down your pale skin.
You held your arms above your head,
as if you could dive upwards into the falls,
your full breasts puckering
to darkest of brown mouths.

We gazed in silence
and then crept away.
You looked like a woman
we'd never seen,
fey and mischievous,
your legs fused,
all silver flow.

Prisoner of War
In memory of my grandfather

When he got home to Ireland in 1945,
he stayed up all night talking,
and then never spoke
of it again, captive
until he died.

What he'd seen, unspeakable. Three years of slaving
on a diet of slugs and rice, hewing a railway
through the mountain jungle of Siam,
its heat and monsoon slime,
along the river Kwai.

No news for 18 months, until a Red Cross postcard:
I am interned at the War Prisoners Camp in (blank).
I am well/not well/in hospital.
From (blank).
Postmarked
in Thai.

When reunited with his eleven-year-old son,
whom he'd last seen aged seven, he shook
the boy's hand. They remained
virtual strangers
all their lives.

The wounds on his back would suppurate for years,
as would his loathing of the Japanese
and his remoteness, fed
—it's said now—
by guilt at having
survived.

He never spoke the litany, but it is written:
dysentery, malaria, beri-beri, lice,
forced labor, beatings, stench.
Our family inheritance—
the roar of hunger,
silence.

His children knew never to spurn any food
on their plates, but his first grandchild
one day stopped speaking and began
to starve herself, as if, unconsciously,
to honor him. Bones strained
up through her skin, death
donning shape before
his eyes.

Maybe the great-grandchildren will bear the damage
lightly, will not be scarred by distant fathers.
Still, they'll know the camp names:
those forgotten places—Chungkai,
Kinsaiyok, Non Pladuk—
where men died
like flies.

The shards of war work blindly
through the flesh of family,
buried shrapnel rising
to the light.

Some Unspeakable Things

1

My quicksilver brother
built himself a fortress that's been breached.
Sometimes, he weeps.

A pulmonologist, he studies
the molecular economy of wasting
in fish, while wasting away himself,
flesh and hunger slipping from him, leached
by some unnameable grief.

The cancer patients he attends
die regularly, fighting to breathe.

2

Once, he flogged me with a fishing rod.
The pain of that first lash
was so large, it exceeded my lungs.
Paralyzed, galvanized,
I couldn't breathe.
That's when I learned
the unspeakable existed.

But I was worse:
once, in a lightning spurt of rage,
I hurled a giant hardback
at his head, felling him with it.

Once, a cobble bit a divet
from the soft chink in his knee.
Blood welled in the hole.
To console him, our mother read
from the *Thousand and One Nights*.

3

When I think of that now,
it has the luminosity of the lost,
like his pure, high, distant voice
leading the choristers in

through the dark church
for midnight mass,
or the time our father took me fishing:
Cork harbor in a little boat with oars,
an outboard motor and a bag of maggots.
I hummed as he fiddled with line and floats,
lulled by his competent baiting, casting,

reeling in, until up reared
a flailing mackerel—
tiger of striped silver
muscle, filling the boat
with its crazed thrashing,
distress crashing in.

I don't know what I'd been expecting:
fish the inert ingredient, perhaps.
Or a decorous, quiet death.
Not this mad fighting, these wild throes.
Maybe I assumed it would die
before it surfaced, the hook a silent bullet.
I'd never pondered how a live
fish became dead and edible.
I begged him to let it go.
Brutal, impatient, he bashed
the beast's head on the side of the boat.
The blood was so bright,
like armfuls of carnations.

4
We ate its body later,
beheaded, disemboweled.
And I enjoyed the eating,
translated to the safe scent of butter foaming
in the iron frying-pan.

5
That year, I took up starving,
wasting away, refusing to speak,

while hunger gnawed me to the bone,
immured in a pure, bleak place,
behind a wall that barred
even my brother.

6

Later, I, too, took up singing.
Later, I came to prize
the pungent, oily, breathless flesh.

.

As If

As if we were still so deep in love as if
the seas had not ganged dry or sands run on
and you and I stood locked together on that cliff
with skylarks burbling in the blue beyond
your eyes a deeper hue drowning and drinking
one another in this one interminable kiss
sun-dazzle spangling sea below
a cup of sky our tears unshed sea pinks
a sweet breeze blowing and your face unlined
and all our years unlived drink from this cup
of eyes sky sea and lips and time will stop
our fears unrealized the dregs of rancor
still undrained and still that summer's day
we two enfolded blended melting fused

Still Day Here

My father writes to me about his day.
Three pages of white vellum
ruled on both sides with his cramped,
incisive words in black ball point pen.

It is a cloudy, humid, still day here...
Not long ago I lost a baby, quit my job.
This morning in a heavy, spattering rain,
leaves dropping from the sodden trees,
cold water dripping down my neck,
I walked to the garage, a cave
of muddy tools and gloves,
bulbs and bikes and hanging ropes,
thin and yellow, dangling from a beam.
Stared at them, stared at the winding sheets of rain
and walked back to the mailbox
where I found this letter.

We're still waiting for the leaf-fall...
If he were here, he'd be expressionless;
a tall man, square and stiff, unbending.
One time he was impaled upon a tree,
Christ-like, except he clambered down
with half a tree branch in his back; walked into town
like Banquo's ghost, all bloody.
Never shed a tear.

I'm digging a new rose bed,
he writes, *beside the lavender bush.*
I see him digging eighteen inches deep, hauling
new black soil to fill it, load by load;
smell the fire he's lit with holly leaves
and thorny skeletons of roses past,
and know for once he's sent me what I need:
within the letter's measured language
chronicling his tending of the place,
is his map for me, his poem.
Look, he's saying, *look:*
This is your home.

Two

Outlander

Being Here

You look like somebody from Belsen,
my parents told me violently, back then.
I just knew I grew purer with each pound less:
pure and light was what I wanted to be.

Hunger the knife, the dog,
the vulture at my gut,
the shadow always at my back.

Just standing was a struggle, sometimes.
And so were the stares—
the shunning stares of strangers
avid to root and feed
upon misfortune, as if I were
the village leper.

Shopkeepers' eyes would shift
from mine and slide away
on smiles and false heartiness.

But I'm here now, despite the black holes,
come back three times from beyond memory,
washed up, still breathing, on the everyday,
tubes battened to my sex and arm,
no choice but to begin again.

A rough-faced nurse sits knitting by my side.
The night light in the passage burns dull blue.
I cannot speak.
She peels a grapefruit and puts it gently,
piece after piece,
into my mouth.
She teaches me to eat the bitter fruit.

Expats

In 1959, my mother is boarding a plane at Heathrow,
her first one ever. She's 23 and newly wed. In the hold
of the BOAC flight to Lagos, changing in Rome,
is her trousseau: the new sheer nightgown,
Liberty print blouses, dirndl skirts, bikini and perfume.
She's wearing the fawn coat she bought
to look wifely, unsure what that might mean.
A green girl, brooding, vulnerable, uncertain—
her hidden stubborn core will see her through.
She is leaving behind everything she knows:
shabby, strait-laced, market-town East Anglia,
her widowed mother and a sister married to a farmer,
her job as typist for a quantity surveyor; the wheat-fields,
gardens, fens and hedgerows of home.

A twist of doubt and fear: his phone call
on the morning of their wedding—did he mean
to call it off, but lost his nerve?
It could all have foundered: when he flew in on leave
to marry her, she went to meet him at the airport,
but arrived too late and found no one. He'd gone on,
desolate, to London, convinced she wouldn't come.
I exist because she found him at the central bus depot.

She's packed a photo of them exiting the church,
wind in her veil. They both look tense.
Perhaps it's terror. Heaven knows. She grips
his arm and will not let him go.
Ahead of her, Nigeria: flights to Kaduna, Jos,
the long Land Rover ride to Gwoza. The rains
will not have finished and the track will be deep mire.
What she'll most remember, later: how
dark and strange the nights were, thrumming
with innumerable unfamiliar insects;
sleeping on camp beds, under mosquito nets.
Three decades later, they drive me to Heathrow
to say goodbye, as, bearing a layer of wedding cake,
I board a flight into my own unknown.

This Is the Blue

This is the blue I fell in love with,
oh, sky of America,
your mornings, your noons, your ineffable dusks,
unclouded, pure and simple,
the color of hope, of surety and thanksgiving,
with space for it all, for new beginnings.
I chose you, flawless and brazen,
clean-slate blue, weightless,
free of freight, for you announced:
I mean just what I say.
Lay down your grief,
your fear, your guilt.
Be joyful.

I come from a huddle of islands,
cloud-cobbled, channel strung,
crowded with accents and tongues,
where the sky is milk-soft and mutable,
unpredictable, tight-fisted.
Where no talk is innocent.
Where speech sets each apart,
indelible marks of class, war,
clan. The weight of history.
Woad. Whisperings.

This is the blue I fell in love with,
oh, north Atlantic off Cape Cod.
The shock of you, green-gray-blue,
shifting cathedral depths, shafted
with grainy light like organ pipes,
singing for striped bass and bluefish,
whelks and crabs. Ocean blue,
I couldn't stay away from you,
crawling the bay six times a day.

This is the blue I fell in love with,
oh, lapis silk of my one-and-only ballgown.
A week I spent cutting and sewing,
stitching up dreams and infatuation,

shipwrecked, of course. It wasn't
the dress's fault. In America,
I chose the color cobalt
for my first down coat, glowed
warm in the searing cold.
I wore it to walk into town
to meet the man I married.
That day it was minus 39,
and the sky was Miró blue.

This is the blue I fell in love with,
oh, garden I planted
here in America: Virginia bluebells,
morning glory, Jacob's ladder,
lupine, salvia, speedwell, squill.
The blue of your eyes, oh my father,
brother, sister, husband, son.
Your changing depths and hues.
Yours, my father, of English forget-me-not,
of prairie indigo, my son,
and yours, my husband,
cyan like the sea you came from,
the ocean you love, the ocean
we always return to.

Wisconsin Wedding Party

I took a quiet road that afternoon,
a weekend city cyclist following
the river's course through corn and soy
and on the way I came across a woman
clad in royal blue polyester, standing alone
in the concrete forecourt of a small town bar,
her face alight with happiness,
waving at the stout, retreating backs
of a wedding party being borne away,
full of hilarity, on a hay wagon,
bride and groom standing up front
behind a tractor belching diesel fumes.

They took my route and there was
no turning back, so I kept pedaling
slowly on behind them, in the wake
of laughter fizzing bright and guileless
as champagne. The tractor chugged along,
relentless as the river, pulling them home
in their tuxedos and bright dresses.

Even at the time, it all felt mythic,
cinematic; something about the light
and the cries seemed to echo from the past,
like old footage from a videocam,
the hazy gold September light haloing the scene,
framing their figures, a Merchant-Ivory shot
of Hardy's Wessex. Which made me think
what tragedies might lie ahead—
the slow, relentless pace of farming life,
the sinew-cracking struggle of it. Imagine him
muck-spreading in the freezing cold.
Imagine the marriage going wrong;
milk prices falling, incest, abuse, adultery,
infections, accidents, machinery failing,
hail, blight, drought, wilt, flood, debt, ruin.

But the tractor simply steamed ahead,
widening the gap between us, cresting

over the hills. My last sight of them:
the bride, erect and willowy, her white veil
streaming out behind, a Chagall vision at the helm
of a hay wagon plowing into the future,
into the mad, brave foolishness of marriage.

Drafting

Headwind on bikes—
there's nothing like it,
hunkered down,
half-blind and deafened, muscle burn
in calves, thighs, forearms,
miles from home.
Try drafting me, you said.
Just ride as close behind me as you can.
It's taken all these years to learn.
I was too busy raging at the wind
and you, always ahead,
afraid that you would hit
an unseen pothole, gravel, a solitary stone;
your swerve or momentary slack
making my wheel kiss yours, us both
careening down, gashed limbs and broken bones.
I chose to battle with the wind alone.
And yet, one day, I find it's almost easy, after all,
to ride a half-wheel span behind you, match
my cadence to your own, your hips
a magnet that I strive towards,
a pendulum of constancy,
the balance delicate—
too near, too far, a back and forth.
Through years of journeying
with you, I've learned
it's worth the pain,
in riot of high wind,
to pull and close the gap, for your back,
broad as a draught horse,
forges me a lee,
a lull,
a breathing space.
Just stay the distance,
close.

Light Traveler

The four-ounce Arctic tern
mates for life,
flies for thirty years
from pole to pole
and back, breeding
in the Arctic summer,
then following the sun
south to Antarctica.

A lifetime of double summers,
drenched in daylight—
endlessly on the wing,
this wind-rider who lives
for voyaging, who stops ashore
only to begin new life,
who's most at home in transit,
flying the equivalent of
three round-trip voyages
to the moon.

What Men Want

Women, when they get together, grouse
about how baffling men are—
how they won't talk, which sticks in the craw—
chewing and working the tough,
unpalatable skin of the world,
till it is supple enough
to be worn.

I think of my husband, mute
on the phone to me, out in the rain,
repainting his dying father's name
on the sign so people could find
their way to his home.

I think of my father, besieged
by work, bending to caress
his roses, breathing in the scent
of blooms named after breeders' wives:
deep crimson *Ena Harkness,*
pure white *Madame Hardy.*

His favorite, a pale yellow flushed
with pink, extremely fragrant,
was called *Peace.*

Thrift

I'd be lying if I said I haven't thrived on silence.
I have steeped in it. I've grown

luxurious and intricate as peonies,
flourished in its loamy soil.

Dear words I never spoke: forgive me.
For a long time, I could feel you

thronging, all of you, quivering.
How you wanted to roar sometimes,

full throttle—babble, prattle, tell your tales,
hold forth, regale, take center stage.

But I chose silence. And now I find
that it has thrived on me. Its fruit has stained

me irremediably. It's grown on me
like Old Man's Beard, while you, poor words,

were filing quietly out backstage, one by one.
From practicing hermetics I've grown

taciturn, each day more clotted.
My word-thriftiness has left me poor.

You are the loss on which I brood.
The miser risks forfeiting all.

Hummingbird

I will not forget the summer I forced myself
out onto the deck and slumped there in despair,
swollen-eyed, slatternly, my throat raw,
my head heavy with drugs that made me
endlessly sleep and eat but did not cure my pain,

how you suddenly appeared, suspended
in mid-air, a jeweled messenger
on wings of living, iridescent green.
The ruby at your throat glowed in the sun
as our eyes met. No one else saw you.

I knew your message was yourself: green
flame of concentrated life, scrap of pure,
unbounded energy. The next time I labored
under the same weight, you reappeared:
hovering between the lilacs and the bleeding heart.

The Bargain

Unsex me then, Celexa, Zoloft, Paxil,
Prozac, Pamelor, Effexor, Lexapro:

stern priestesses, vestal virgins,
make my quietus. Fix me. Extinguish

agony awhile, excise the mass
of sadness on my solar plexus.

Halt the flaying, grant me sleep,
give me my skin back, let me speak.

And I will pay you what you ask.
Come claim your pound of flesh.

Come douse my small, blue pilot light, my luxury,
my hum, my buzz, my fizz, my calyx.

I offer you my fig, my nub, my sap, my wick.
Make me a cipher, an amputee, a cicatrix.

No more this tinder, this tender and this flint,
this suffuse and swell, this flare, this fierce,

this fill, this fuse, this fusion,
this cleaving to, this cleft, these two.

The Breath of Houses

The breath of houses here is often sweet.
Sometimes, at dusk, they exhale

a waft of laundry, baking, wood-smoke.
A lone walker sees through their lit windows

a family at table, an old man reading,
a woman kneeling to lay logs in a fireplace,

a schoolgirl practicing the piano.
The walker sees her own breath on the air.

Why is it that at nightfall, other people's lives
seem so inviting, so untroubled, so secure?

Maybe the kid stumbling through "Für Elise"
is losing herself the only way she knows;

the old man is reading his oncology report;
the woman kneeling has quarreled with her son

and has arthritis in her hands, which hurt;
the father called his lover before dinner.

Still, the central heating purrs. Meals occur.
There is milk. There are warm beds to sleep in

and clean clothes, in these our only,
our miraculous, our onion-scented homes.

To My Parents on the Day of the Dead

You're perfectly fine,
but I've been noticing
you walk more slowly now uphill,
it takes you forever to read
fine print,
and your house
has started to smell
orderly and tranquil,
like the houses
of your parents.

I've begun to fear your death.
When I've been swimming in the sun
a spasm of remembered dread runs through me
at the thought of winter,
how it will come on
no matter what.

Today, as I rake the last leaves
beneath the mulberry tree,
I remember what you told me about leaf mold;
how the old leaves make potent soil,
how their dead bodies
nourish new seeds.

I lean on the rake and look up.
This is the first time
I've seen how dying
clarifies. Now all the leaves
are gone, I can see out and up,
with no obstructions.

Arctica Islandica

1

Seeing the ice, congealing like white fat
on the dark stock of the pond, I think
of the four-hundred-and-five-year-old clam
just dredged from the Arctic Ocean
north of Iceland. Quahog *Arctica Islandica*,
the oldest living creature ever found,
born the year the English landed on Cape Cod
and William Shakespeare wrote *Othello*,
three when *Don Quixote* hit the press,
seven when Galileo peered through
his first ever telescope. In those cold
and pristine seas it drifted, larval, landed
upon velvet silt and burrowed in,
growing a film of shell a year. Daily,
it sipped a slow rain of plankton.
Global warming researchers from Wales
sawed, unsuspecting, through its small,
drab and unremarkable shell to tell
its age, counting its rings like a tree's.
An unfortunate aspect of our work
was that the clam died.

2

I once worked eight years in the deep
Midwest at a job I hated, in a town known only
for the invention of barbed wire and GM corn.
The Chicago and Northwestern Railroad ran
right through it. Freight trains
woke me at ungodly hours, wailing
like banshees, long into the seamy night,
shaking the floorboards and the raddled
window sashes in the clapboard houses.

3

The last glacier of the last
Ice Age passed through the city
I live in now, scouring all beneath.
Just west of here, it stopped.
The country beyond has hilltops,

views, variety, a sense of perspective.
To us, the glacier bequeathed the plain,
the sand and clay I wrestle with
each summer, planting annuals.
Ten thousand years have passed
and still, this far north, winter
is a spiritual exercise, weight-
training for the soul.

4

The Roto-Rooter man tries doggedly
but fails to fix the trammeled drain.
He blames it on the trees,
their greedy roots. Sober
for twelve years, he says,
he's gone back to the drink.
Was it the blizzard? I think,
the freezing rain?
Too many drains?
After that visit he vanishes,
answers no more calls.

5

My son, five, wants to know
why God, who could choose to make us
live forever, lets us die.
It's not kind of Him, he reasons, puzzled,
beginning to be aggrieved.

6

I know Tylenol and temperatures and loose teeth.
I know mounds of corn snow and blebbed ice.
I know whitegraybrown.
I know Christmas lights
in the dark. I know
chapped lips.

7

A ten-year-old in Mexico
glues his hand to the bedstead

after Christmas, not wanting
the humdrum life of school.

8

That clam and I have things in common:
the drabness of our lives,
the cold, the hidden muscle.
I am reminded of him when the snows
keep falling and I weep over onions,
endlessly load the dishwasher,
endlessly wipe the counters with a dirty cloth,
do endless laundry and find underpants
and fix holes in knees. As I clean
cat vomit and hairballs.
Contemplate my small living room,
endlessly choked by toys.

I know thickened.
I know a slowed heart.
I know hunger expanding.

9

I want marigolds and mangoes.
I want lambs keeping me awake
with their bawling and celandines
on old airfields and the valleys opening.
I want woods full of bluebells.
I want the mountains of North Wales:
Moel Siabod, Cadair Idris, Tryfan.

I want figs and custard apples.
I want thyme on the hillsides
and lemons on the trees.
I want to go back to that place in Spain
called "Birth of the River World."

I want a Welsh men's choir
with a thunderous golden organ
to fell me, belting out "Cwm Rhondda"
like the crowds at rugby matches:
Bread of Heaven, Bread of Heaven,
Feed me till I want no more (want no more)
Feed me till I want no more.

10

I open and inhale saffron, desiring
everything to be yellow, orange, red.
All winter, I cook foods from abroad.
Fry olive oil, turmeric and sweet paprika,
sweat shallots. I cook basmati
brown rice, purple, white. Roast squash
in oil of French hazelnuts
till carmelized. Grate ginger root.
Split green cardamom, pour
coconut milk. Chop feta cheese
and dill. Simmer broth
of miso, shiitake, kelp.

11

I listen to the shipping forecast
for the British Isles:
Dogger, Fisher, Viking, German Bite,
Rockall, Shannon, Fastnet, Lundy,
Irish Sea. South wind veering west later,
gale force eight, occasional showers, rain.

12

Growing up near Wales, I never listened
to Welsh men's choirs. I only noticed
how barren and poor the life was:
rain on slate roofs, slag heaps,
the mountains bleak and shrouded.
I never noticed with what joy
they could sing of hardship,
ordinariness, endurance.

I never expected
happiness, *pilgrim*
in this barren land.
This barren, rich life.
Our unremarkable existences,
with their secret, iridescent insides.

Three

Bloodroot

Bloodroot

Outside the music teacher's house, this
first brownish thrust of live leaf from dead,
this native spring ephemeral, so
unlike its primal, sexy name that conjures
up our genesis: man's hard root
plunged in its furrow, the birth cord
snaking from the blood-rich placenta.

Bloodroot is Easter Week, the Paschal lamb,
Bach and the Passions,
string consorts on their period instruments
wringing sounds from sheep gut,
bitter myrrh and torture,
death and resurrection,
the waning and waxing
of this world decaying, budding,

is the house finches returning,
expectant, with their complex,
liquid song, the robins'
cheeriup, cheeriup, cheerio,
box-elder bugs making out on the front step,
coyote scat in the park, a rabbit's nest, old
honeycomb in the grass,

is magnolia in bud, a few
musky cream cups leaking their green,
veiled scent, or my neighbor, 102,
who goes out weekly to play bridge,
and the ambulance that pulls up
outside her house, lights flashing,
but then leaves without her,

is the red-garbed cardinal intoning
too, too few, few, few.

Onset

My mother dreams a journey with my dad.
En route, he goes, they both think, to the men's room,
which turns out to be a train

that leaves the station with him on board,
holding it all: passports, tickets, visas, money,
address of destination.

"Tell me," Dad says to our host
for the third time tonight, "Have you ever been
to the Far East?" He gets lost now

coming back from the bathroom at night.
She wakes at three to find him sleepless, floored.
"Whose house is this? How did we get here?"

"America, America," she soothes.
"We're in America." "I know," he snaps, "but . . .
whose car did we come in?"

By day there is a vague sadness to him,
something muffled, absent, subdued. No flares.
No more tearing up the lists

she makes him,
or hurling the shreds
to the floor.

Maple Keys

The fruits of the silver maple
have arrived, winged hordes of them,
helicoptered in. They lie in wait
on the front porch, infiltrate
the bedroom on our shoes.

It rains for three weeks straight.
The world is a ripe, gray womb.
Pairs of minute, rust-tinged leaves
with silver maple teeth
begin appearing everywhere.

Each seedling bears a pair
of molted wings, whose nub
has sprung a taproot down into the soil,
a straight shoot up towards the sun.

They will take anywhere—
beds, gutters, cracks in concrete.
I uproot dozens every day
and still they come.

I used to think
conception was this easy,
that the challenge was to bar the way
to all those million sperm.

I chart my seasons, wet and dry,
wonder if a single seed
will lodge and root in me.
When did the odds against a human
seedling come to seem so high?

With Child

1

Every month the echographers
pored over the mound with their probes,
inscribing it with loops, flourishes,
question marks, in their invisible ink.
Intent on their work, digging in till it hurt,
as if I were a wax tablet,
blank for their scrawls.
Sound waves trawled the depths
of intercellular space, struck moonscapes
beamed back to the black
and white TV by the bed. Conjurers
of unreality, they'd produce scrolls of pictures
and hand them to me to take home:
tadpole, seahorse, white-haired Neptune.

There's evidence that babies
practice crying in the womb
as well as acrobatics.
They're busy in there. So much
to do, to prepare.

2

Six weeks out.
Seasick.

3

My contours blur, shift,
morphing. Becoming
us. Mystery
and obliteration.
Emerging.
My stomach has grown
elbows. It can have hiccups
for hours.

4

I start wearing whatever
fits. I no longer choose

fabrics, cuts, colors; women
leave black trash bags
full of hand-me-downs
on our porch.
My own style vanishes.
People say
pregnancy becomes me.

5

Elderly prima gravida
the doctors termed me: grave matter
bearing your first child
after forty. Gravity
calls. The grave.
The engravers.

6

I wrote almost nothing
of it. It was too great
a state of flux, too
momentous and mundane.
Only this, found later:
one loose page, undated:

Long dark mornings:
sleeping weather.
Baby twitching,
stomach growing.
There is a plague of ladybugs
in here. What do they live on,
buzzing around all winter long,
drunk on light,
on white snow light?

7

I went swimming daily with my also-pregnant friend.
Towards the end, encumbered as astronauts,
we were only comfortable when floating.
Our bellies preceded us like spinnakers
running before the wind. The pool
was liberation—laps, flip turns
and dolphin kicks away from gravity,
girdles, support hose, piles of grimy snow.

8

She wanted a portrait of herself
pregnant, underwater, in the deep end.
With no zoom lens and our ballooning
bodies forging always up,
the camera's frame could not encompass
more than her bulbous torso, ripe plum
ready to drop. Her head and long,
slim limbs kept straying out.
I could never hold my breath
enough to get a single picture right.
But I shot the whole roll, thinking
at least we'd have bits and pieces of her,
something to show what pregnancy
was like. In the end, all thirty-six photos
came out blank.

9

The child inhabits you
like a whelk the whorls of its shell,
a hidden smile. At some level,
you are always intimately
accompanied, like holding
a lover's hand
everywhere you go.

First Family Portrait

Here is a close-up of the moment after
your body slithered in a sudden rush from mine,
white frog on my chest. Giddy laughter
illuminates the room, release from nine
long hours of labor. Sweaty and sunken-eyed,
I look delighted—a surprise, since at the time
I just felt stunned. Your mouth is open wide,
your father's face alight; we three a pantomime
of the Nativity—but look how many nameless arms
are twined around this mortal scrap, look how
you landed in this woven limb-nest, caught by luck
in the one safety net the human race can offer,
the net you leapt into at birth, far stronger
than your parents, stumbling numb toward love.

After Birth

People walk around on the streets
as if nothing had happened.
Coming back from the hospital
I feel as if I'd just been born
myself, everything seems so strangely
familiar. The strangeness makes me weep.
There are traffic lights still. The same
florist on the corner. The same streets.
The same sidewalks. When we get home
we lie down together in silence,
out of the cruel sun.
The neighbors' dog barks in the back yard.
"That is a dog," I tell you.
"That is the first dog you have ever heard.
You will get to know him well." The trees
have greened during my two days away
with tiny, round, chartreuse
explosions, maple flowers.

Wellspring

This is the milk

        of humankind/ness

              thin   tepid

    bluish   sweet

my breasts hum   spurt

        burn me

     as they feed you

one cry   and I

     am drenched

milk forms   in the deep

      dark   chthonic heat

            where poems

      come from

    you grow fat

on it alone

Oxygen

She could have survived
without milk that long.
She was old enough.
Six months
is old enough.
It wasn't the heat.
It was the air.
The windows were
sealed shut sealed
so tight she just
ran out of air.

Her eyes were open,
but she couldn't see.

There were red
maple leaves all over
the windshield, the warm
wind blowing them
everywhere.

Man in a Parking Lot

When you have a son
you start seeing men
backwards, intuiting their childhood
selves beneath the years of accretions—
the bags and jowls, paunches,
thickened, crumpled skin,
the whole weight of the individual
personality, its freight of filters,
opinions, prejudices, habits,
likes, congealed—as if you knew them
before they even knew themselves.

So when a man stumbles toward you,
mumbling, across the Safeway parking lot,
unkempt and coatless in the snow,
and your discriminating mind says
"madman," "danger," though he never
once looks up, locked in an altered world,
fixed, unfixable, you lock your car door and then
sit there wondering how it happened,
when things started going wrong.
Knowing he was once a toddler,
for pity's sake, you find it
strange, unreal, this mane of wild
gray hair, gray beard. Somehow,
you know it doesn't belong on him,
all that hair, and you don't know
how he got to be so lost, so sick, so old.

On Seeing Anna Karenina

Once, I was an expert on realism
in the nineteenth-century novel. Thousands
of pages read and annotated till my eyes
blurred and my hand ached and my head swam
with scenes from other worlds: St. Petersburg,
Rouen, Madrid, Vetusta, Middlemarch.
I considered Anna K. from many angles—feminist,
New Critical, historical—her world
so intimate she seemed like family.

And yet I leave the movie curiously shaken,
pierced by what, for years, I overlooked:
the doomed, defenseless figure at the center of the whirl
is not Anna after all, bewitching as she is.
It's not the lovers, with their self-indulgent agonies
and ecstasies; not steely, bloodless, cuckolded Karenin;
not Levin yearning earnestly to marry Kitty,
with all his pious claptrap about peasant life.

It's little Seryozha—Anna's son.

The scenes of her stooping to his bedside,
kissing a flawless, sleeping cheek, inhaling
while planning to abandon him, sear me,
unbearable.
                    With shock, I realize
that something in me was forever altered
by the firestorm of labor and delivery.
I was reborn. I see things differently.
I had it wrong, and so did all the realists:
a son's not marginal, a backdrop
to the main events. The scent
of his skin, breath, hair: that's passion,
that's what's real.

Kite

You fell in love with it at Ace Hardware,
tawdry plastic triangle emblazoned
with a Warner Brothers bear whirling
up out of a tornado, arms akimbo, snarling
teeth and huge pink tongue. We balked
at the price, $3.59 for a sheet of flimsy plastic,
four dowels the size of straws, cord
thin as sewing thread. With your small-boy
yen for things flamboyant and cartoon,
you wept for it, so we paid up
and went to fly it.
                              The riot wind
felt good, warm enough for shorts,
too strong for wasps, mosquitos, no-see-ums.
In the park, the urgent cries of soccer teams,
children shrieking on the slide. Wisps of cirrus
overhead, banked storm clouds moving in.
You wanted to let it out as far as it would go
and you were right. Low down, it kept on veering
into nose dives, tangling with trees, but at 100 yards
the current started, unseen high road.
The kite sensed it, child yearning at a gate
to another world. Up there it came alive,
giant tiger moth, quivering, eager, wild.
We passed it back
                              and forth, you and I,
lying by the lake behind the ice-cream store.
Wind and water, grass and cloud, ground and sky.
It felt like fishing, braced against such strength,
the kite anchored on the wind, straining
to leave, yet steady at its distance, tethered
for now, like you to me, like both of us
to earth.

Gardening

There's that frisson
of sacrilege when the spade
first slices in—dry sound,
rank smell, trespass—your blade
bisecting topsoil, loam, worms, grubs,
mulch, the whole flecked earth full
of roots, corms, seeds, spores, rhizomes,
all in wait, programmed
to begin becoming.

You get to play God.
You decide who lives, who dies,
who goes where and when.
Who gets plenty to eat and drink.
Who is good, bad, beautiful.
Who gets uprooted, dumped.

On the seventh day, you stop,
survey your work, satisfied.
You get lazy again. In time,
you will resent the most successful,
especially the fecund immigrants,
the invasives—goutweed, dame's rocket,
dandelion, honeysuckle, tansy—who thrive
and crowd the natives out.

So much hope each spring, forking
through white skeins of goutweed,
wresting wiry black dandelion
sinews out of the flinty clay.
So much earthwork.
And in the end, so much defeat.
They always win, the plants:
they'll bury your plans
and go their own way.

The Dogs of Love

I hear him crowing on the wooden fort,
the boy my mild son worships like a brother,
hear him taunting and my child's faint answer
from below, defensive, sounding hurt.
Something in the air has shifted. A cry,
repeated. Impatiently, I trudge around to see.
My child is weeping, laced with the other's pee,
dark ribbons on his hair and shirt, while I
am speechless. Visions of my own best friend
whispering to us girls once, "Let's be men
and piss on that wall." When I demurred they swore,
ranks closed, claws out, street-tough.
How savagely we punish difference, weakness, love.
And yet we keep on going back for more.

Psalm

I pause in the airport parking ramp, alive
with the avid conversations of sparrows
celebrating the ordinary.

They make this half-deserted hangar
musical as a cathedral, open to the air,
full of light and shadow, cool spaces.

I see our house when it was a great skeleton
of yellow wood, the roof ribs of whale,
green glow of summer in the rafters.

A wasp's nest falls from the heft
of the silver maple. I hold
this fine gray paper from the sky.

I sing and sometimes sound fills
my mouth and throbs there, my throat
an instrument, my ribs a soundboard.

I swim, keeping my head low
in the water, thinking of scals:
breathe, swivel, drive, flip, glide.

I endure the clamor of children,
ground down smooth by it like shingle,
clattered and worn on the strand.

I plant wormwood, sage.
I snap asparagus spears,
split the wood from the green.

The mock orange that I tried to kill
is drenched in blossom, tipsy.
Again, its scent undoes me.

Her Guide to Household Management

Jumbo-sized kitchen roll. Make jam.
Dredge day's accumulated debris nightly.
Dream. Pledge to detach.
3lbs organic chicken breasts and thighs,
bone-in but skinless. Vacuum
and mop floors. Closet errant boots,
coats, hats, trains, gloves and underwear.
Cloister. Chronicle.
Change sheets. *Snatch sleep.* Bleach out
dried blood and pawmarks.
Muse. Gaze. Jot notes on Post-its.
Buy Clifford the Big Red Dog Band-Aids.
Return library books (16), pay fine on "Passion
According to St Matthew." Something
on hold. But what?
Hoard solitude. Get Valentine. *Be wolfish.*
Dig deep. Defend your lair.
Raspberry fruit leather.
Wrangle. Tooth and claw.
5 loads of wash on warm, mixed colors.
Root out those scarlet chenille socks
that always run. Do not forget.
Ramble. Lavish.
3 medium leeks. Make soup.
Tomato ketchup. Honey for tea, sore throats
and bribery. Bread flour.
Loaf. Laze. Linger.
Ext. virgin olive oil. Ajax. Kix.
Expand. Crave ecstasy.
Scrub grime off bath and sink.
Skimp. Stint. Survive.
Get sitter Tuesday night (?).
Braid. Weather. Soften.
Steep in stillness.
Rinse with light.

Excavation

Devouring earth for a new highway,
the dozers spat out skulls.

Don't worry: this is not
a horror story. No violence

was done; they were ancient
Gauls, peacefully interred.

The archeologists were sent for,
given a summer to unearth

what they could from the sun-baked plain.
That's how I came, a volunteer,

to spend a month brushing teeth.
Skulls lack noses, so the ground,

as we scraped laboriously away,
began to sprout jawbones,

a field of cracked and dusty teeth,
from which no men would spring.

I think of them sometimes,
brushing my son's milk teeth nightly—

the same age, roughly, as the child
sown in soil I spent so long uncovering.

Elementary School

Weekdays at seven a.m., we're at the crossroads
waiting with our children for the yellow bus.
There is no shelter and no place to sit,
as if to stress the point of schooling
is not comfort, but exposure.
An odd assortment of adults—
the trial lawyer, the nurse, the electrician,
the unemployed, the pregnant with her fourth,
the newly arrived from Chicago, the secretary,
and two days a week the divorced father
from the other side of town—all of us variously
sullen, chipper, sleepy, shy, close-mouthed.

The first day of school, we eyed each other
with suspicion, tribal. Now
we share the cameraderie of strangers
traveling together: wary bonhomie,
some friendships. Daily,
we put a good face on our private chaos,
chivvy or bully our kids out the door,
dressed or dressing, disheveled, brushed,
the stragglers and the punctual,
nurse our coffee while the children tussle
on the corner, high-voiced like stars.

The bus roars up. They form a ragged line,
clamber aboard bearing their ludicrously
heavy packs, their inadequate, cobbled-together
lunches. Some child always turns at the door,
urgent: "Wave to me!" and all the parents
stand there as the bus pulls off, waving,
though the tinted windows, twelve black oblongs,
are so dark we can't tell if our kids
can see us waving, if they're waving back,
or where they sit, or who they journey with,
whether they're sad, content, indifferent,
oblivious—but we keep on waving,
united in this instant of pure,
absurd devotion, till they're gone.

Aubade
For my mother-in-law

Four thirty-two a.m. She lies awake,
listening to the even breath
of the Atlantic and her husband
in the next bed. Some day soon,
his breathing will not be there.
This knowledge is what woke her.
Raised on the northwest coast,
she came east after the war,
was wooed and wed within a year.
Her island childhood was rougher,
wilder, freer, not at all like this.
She found his family daunting:
the men all officers, the chauffeur
and the maid both uniformed,
cocktails at six, raising the flag,
dress for dinner. Her folks
did not visit. In those days, wives
cleaved to their husbands.

Four forty-seven.
The song sparrow starts his
sweet sweet sweet, oh! so very sweet
from the pine tree on the bluff,
generations of song sparrows
on that tree since the house was built.
And now the Carolina wren joins in,
the towhee and the catbird, the goldfinches
she feeds with thistle seed.
The same songs, the same sea
she heard each day, those months
on bed-rest in the upstairs room.

Marigold print curtains bloomed
in the on-shore breeze.
She lay and lay through the sixth,
seventh, eighth, ninth month,
stared at the indefatigable ocean.
Occasionally a biplane or an osprey
would traverse the window, the scent

of box, a whiff of brine and beach rose.
Sweltering heat on still nights.
Some days, the foghorn, and always,
at six a.m., the drone
of the lobsterman's skiff.
Inexorable advance-
retreat of surf.

She'd hear them laughing
over dinner down below.
His brother used to come up
and take tea with her sometimes.
She was so grateful.

Four fifty-five.
The bell buoy on the point
begins to toll; the tide
has turned and she remembers
her first child, born dead,
and the second, yanked
feet first and only just
in time from her.
The third, the one
she had to lie so still to keep,
the sunny one,
is sleeping now
in that same upstairs room
he slept in fifty years ago,
the summer before
he was born.

Lily

I pause before the crayon contour of a lily
by a New York artist with an Irish name.
The line releases and I'm gone,
for what he calls Calla is an Arum
or an Easter lily, and I'm spinning, torn:

the altar lilies, surplice white,
at my son's christening
that spring, in Shropshire;
the farflung family clustered round the font,
a smell of must and stone
with Father Tom intoning.

And down, and down, until
I reel *you* in, father.
Schooled, like MacNeice, *to a foreign voice,*
you come of Planter stock.
Your grandfather a seed merchant in Cork,
a Methodist, dour and tyrannical,
with a small estate and a big house,
which he ruled with an iron thumb.
But you chose a life in England
and all of that's long gone.

You swapped the iron thumb for a green one
and schooled me well on English plants.
I call this lily "Arum," "Lords and Ladies,"
"Cuckoo-Pint," "Jack-in-the-Pulpit,"
because that's what you told me.
You'd kneel to point it out,
wild in the woodlands on our walks,
finger its single, waxen bract.

You said the plant was poisonous.
You knew everything, I thought,
a walking encyclopedia.

Why did you never then reveal this lily's

Irish side as symbol of remembrance
marking the Easter Rising and its dead?

What did you think of all that, anyway—
Ulster in flames, armed squaddies, hunger strikes,
check points, surveillance, bombs, internment camps?
Trips to your parents' house in Ire Land
in those days were often tense, explosive,
but the Troubles never talked of.

How did you manage otherness?
What else have you not told?
I need to know: I too
have crossed the water, even farther.

Too late to ask you now.
Your brain is self-destructing, faulty
connections firing off at random.
But you cling to Ireland through
long nights of grim delusion, like a drowning man
to spars of wreckage, reciting endlessly
your childhood address: *Where do I live now?*
Ferry House, Currabinny, Co. Cork.
A fine place, indeed...Cork Harbor,
sailing boats...now, what is my address? Oh yes...

There are two chaplains at the hospital
and both visit you. The Catholic comes first,
offering Mass: small, lithe, a smoker's
deep-scored countenance, a quick, warm grin.
You light up when he enters, for his speech
is southern Irish. You mention Currabinny
and the man smiles back
and says some words in Gaelic.
A blank. You do not know
a word of Irish, not even hello.
A kinship, then, but also,
still, four centuries on, that tribal gulf:
the Gael from the Anglo-Irish.

You do not take communion
with him but from the other

chap, who's Anglican,
tall, gauche, and plummy,
just like you.
So, each to each.
Aye, there's the rub.

Tell me: how does the heart survive
its transplantation?
Does what is won
ever outweigh the cost?

He makes it seem so simple, Kelly.
One pure line, only one name.
How could he be so sure of how to draw this lily—
Calla, Easter, Arum? I'm still torn—
this funeral flower, whose pale calyx
holds so much: allegiance, country, clan, all hidden
in that creamy spathe with its big, rude spike
that's clad in bright red berries in the woods
in autumn, when the flowering's done.

Solstice Under Snow

December guttering almost to the wick.
The houses shawled, the shrubs white sheaves,
and glittering knives ranged neatly on the eaves.
At pewter dusk, a giant low is wending
east toward us, bearing more snow.
You kiss me goodnight, retire to read
by lamp-light, sip your glimmering peat.
Waking warm in night's long deep,
furled in our feather bed, I know
the snow's slow silt is drifting down,
sifting the buildings with silence up to the sills.
Our house is shingled tight.
Lulled on the steady swell and ebb,
the softly breaking waves of breath—
yours, mine, the cat's—I feel
a coal shift somewhere, suddenly,
and flare, a sudden blaze
of glad to be your kith and kin,
spliced, hitched, in this for life.

Coda

Lineage

I come from tin miners and teetotalers and trawlermen, from shingle coves and mackerel shoals. I come from hill-forts and longships, from railways and runner beans. I come from Huguenots and hooligans, from hamlets on fire, from fields of rape. I come from a smudge of mountains, from stone-throwing and name-calling and terraced houses and no central heat. I come from one bath a week. I come from Cruise missiles and car bombs, from plimsolls and power cuts, from truncheons and typewriters, from Wimpy Bars and 99's and Hovis loaves. I come from the Malvinas, from Marmite and mutton-fat, from gas-masks and gobstoppers, from slag-heaps and shagging. I come from the Downs and the Fens. I come from wrecked galleons and 1066 and an arrow in the eye. I come from Normandy and Flanders, from poppies with plastic stalks and a black plastic heart. From sugar beet and winter wheat, from bracken and rowan and heather on the hills.

•

I come from women who were wide-hipped and milk-lush. I come from pitmen and airmen and rugby players, from runes and Roundheads, Agas and ashes. I come from expats and Elizabeths. I come from upstanding, from esquires. I come from a governess and wolves on the steppes. I come from rationing and the Raj, monsoons and mountaineers, saris and salwar kameez, kippers and kedgeree. I come from Methodists and Marcher lords, from Druids and Danes and Angles, from Offa and Owain Glendŵr. I come from Cornish and Latin, Norse and Norman, Hausa and Urdu and Malay. I come from bryony and bilberries and barley-corn, from barges and bowling greens and bluebells. From towpaths and viaducts, chaffinch and midges, nettles and dock. From sheep-dip and cowpats, stiles and salt-licks, peat fires and Page Three. I come from Greenham Common and Guy Fawkes and the Green Man, from the Black Lion and the Cross Foxes. I come from coppicing and coddled eggs, from woodpigeons and woodlice. I come from conkers and coracles, from cuckoo spit and Spitfires and the Knights Hospitaller. From the Confessor and the Lionheart, from potteries and kilns, from dye-pits and district officers, from thorn fences and all the curs barking.

I come from bards and blast furnaces, from badger setts and Brixton and the Blitz, from baps and butties and boiled cabbage. I come from Ironbridge and iron wills, from knuckle-dusters and the National Front. I come from vicars and vergers, vestries and kestrels, kettles and cobblestones. I come from hurley and hawthorn and hedgehogs and hedgerows. I come from footpaths and frogspawn and drystone walls. I come from birders and botanists, liverwort and otter scat, hankies and hot water bottles. I come from turf-cutters, from bogs and bothies, from graffiti and guinea-fowl. I come from snogging at bus-stops, from smog and smut and soot. I come from teacakes and Toby jugs, from mince pies and marrows, crumpets and scrumpy. I come from last orders and Vindaloos and loos. From Dettol and hard water and chapped hands. From mangles and manor houses and market gardens. From ruined abbeys, from the bones of monks and naves.

•

I come from flotsam and jetsam, from kelp and dabberlocks and bladder wrack, from haddock and herring. I come from cockles and mussels and kittiwakes. I come from ferrymen and foxglove and fuchsia, from Penguin and Puffins. From pilchard pie and sticks of pink-and-white-striped rock. From sunburn and freckles. From rude seaside postcards. From Us and Them. From cuttlebone and Crimplene and stripped pine. From causeways and cagoules and caravan parks, from wherries and skerries, from wellies and Shell Island and camping in the rain.

•

I come from survivors, from serfs and settlers and skinheads, from greengrocers and gallows birds and grave-diggers. I come from poachers and the poll tax. I come from longbows and the lion rampant and the Wars of the Roses. From the Enclosures, the Black Death, the Great Fire, the Dissolution, the Armada, Trafalgar, Waterloo. I come from the stocks. From the mud of the trenches, the Western Front. From beech-bole and trip-wires. From meadow-sweet and lady-smock. From hugger-mugger, from cramped, from pinched, from raw. I come from mummers and morris dancers, from flummery and gooseberry fool. I come from mild, from over-cooked. I come from bell-ringers and bob and bobbies and Bob's your uncle. I come from withy beds and wicker hampers, from moors and meres and motorways, from cart tracks and canal wharves.

•

I come from green thumbs and big bones. I come from gleaners and wreckers, from hand-me-downs, from mongrels, from make-do-and-mend, from sew-your-own. I come from sixpenny bits, from gristle, from darkness, from devil's toenails. I come from ammonites and axe-heads, from mottes and baileys, from wattle and daub. I come from watchers and waiters, from blarney-kissers, from bide-your-timers. From beacons and bunkers. From fords and forges. From slate and flint and schist. From ley lines and long barrows, from dolmens and standing stones, from chapels and cairns, from bedrock and grey light. From lichen. From drizzle. From granite.

NOTES

Bloodroot is a spring-flowering plant native to the eastern half of North America. It has white petals and reddish sap.

"Dis/locations" — Definitions partially derived from *The New Shorter Oxford English Dictionary* (1993). The term **homelooseness** was coined by James Wood in his essay "On Not Going Home" in *The London Review of Books*, Vol. 36 No. 4.

"Passport" — **Hefted** is a term used by farmers in the north of England to describe sheep and other animals' attachment, learned from their mothers, to a particular piece of upland pasture (a "heft"). Once hefted, they will never voluntarily leave the area, so there is no need to fence them when grazing open hill country or moorland.

"Crossing the Welsh Border" — **Araf** means "slow" in Welsh. **Croeso i Gymru** means "Welcome to Wales." **Dinas Brân** is a steep hill outside the town of Llangollen in North Wales; it is the site of an Iron Age hillfort and a ruined medieval castle.

"Viroconium" — The Roman city of **Viroconium**, near Wroxeter in Shropshire, thrived from the 2nd to the 5th century.

"Burial Ground" — This poem describes a *cillín*, one of the many unofficial, unconsecrated burial places for unbaptized children in Ireland. Their use died out in the 1990s.

"Oxygen" — The poem is based on a report in the *Beloit Daily News* (October 10, 2003) about the death by suffocation of a baby unintentionally left in a car all day.

"Lily" — **Planters** is the name given to the British colonists who were brought in to settle land confiscated from the Irish Gaels by the English Crown in the 16th and 17th centuries. The **Easter Lily** is a badge bearing the image of a white lily that is worn at Easter to commemorate the deaths of Irish republican fighters during the struggle for independence since the 1916 Easter Rising in Dublin.

Catherine Jagoe is an award-winning poet, translator and writer based in Madison, Wisconsin. Born in Britain, she lived in England, Nigeria and Spain before moving to the United States in 1988. She holds a doctorate in Spanish literature from Cambridge University, and is the author of two poetry chapbooks, *Casting Off* (Parallel Press) and *News from the North* (Finishing Line Press). ***Bloodroot***, her first full-length collection of poetry, is the winner of the **2016 Settlement House American Poetry Prize**.

The Settlement House American Poetry Prize is awarded annually to a book of poems by a first-generation American poet. The Prize alternates annually between a book written in the language of a poet's ancestry and translated into English and a collection written in English.

For additional information, please visit www.settlementhouse.us.

SETTLEMENT HOUSE POETRY

The Carnival, The Life—David Allan Evans

* *Bloodroot*—Catherine Jagoe

South Pole / Polo Sur—Maria Teresa Ogliastri (translated by Yvette Neisser Moreno and Partricia Bejarano Fisher)

* *Flowering Fires / Fuegos Florales*—Alicia Partnoy (translatedby Gail Wronsky)

King Philip's War—Sheppard Ranbom

The Lunatic in the Trees—Dennis Sampson

Within the Shadow of a Man—Dennis Sampson

As Sunrise Becomes the World: A Trilogy—Louie Skipper

It Was the Orange Persimmon of the Sun—Louie Skipper

The Work Ethic of the Common Fly—Louie Skipper

The Unattended Harp—Peter Waldor

** *Who Touches Everything*—Peter Waldor

The Importance of Being Zimmer—Paul Zimmer

* Settlement House American Poetry Prize
**National Jewish Book Award, 2013

Settlement House Books, Inc., is an independent, non-profit 501 (c)(3) book publisher. Founded in 2007, we take our name from the settlement houses of the late 19th, 20th and current centuries that provided—and continue to provide—community through their social and cultural support and service to the urban poor and immigrant populations. In that spirit, we think of ourselves as a home for some of the fine voices of poetry deserving of greater readership now and in the future.

www.settlementhouse.us